TERRIFIC TEAMS

Meet the CHICAGO CUBS

ZELDA WAGNER

Lerner Publications ◆ Minneapolis

Stats in this book are accurate through the 2024 Major League Baseball season.

Lerner Publications Company
An imprint of Lerner Publishing Group, Inc.
241 First Avenue North
Minneapolis, MN 55401 USA

For reading levels and more information, look up this title at www.lernerbooks.com.

Main body text set in ITC Avant Garde Gothic Std.
Typeface provided by Adobe Systems.

Editor: Elena Mai **Designer:** Martha Kranes

Library of Congress Cataloging-in-Publication Data

Names: Wagner, Zelda, 2000- author
Title: Meet the Chicago Cubs / Zelda Wagner.
Description: Minneapolis, MN : Lerner Publications, [2026] | Series: Terrific teams (Lerner sports rookie) | Includes bibliographical references and index. | Audience: Ages 5–8 | Audience: Grades K–1 | Summary: "After more than 100 years, the Chicago Cubs finally won their third World Series in 2016. From superstars to exciting plays, learn more about the oldest team in the MLB"—Provided by publisher.
Identifiers: LCCN 2025015085 (print) | LCCN 2025015086 (ebook) | ISBN 9798765689660 library binding | ISBN 9798348029425 paperback | ISBN 9798765699300 epub
Subjects: LCSH: Chicago Cubs (Baseball team)—History—Juvenile literature | Major League Baseball (Organization)—History—Juvenile literature
Classification: LCC GV875.C6 W34 2026 (print) | LCC GV875.C6 (ebook) | DDC 796.357/640977311—dc23/eng/20250520

LC record available at https://lccn.loc.gov/2025015085
LC ebook record available at https://lccn.loc.gov/2025015086

Manufactured in the United States of America
1-1012407-54834-5/23/2025

Photo Acknowledgments
Image credits: AP Photo/Paul Beaty, p. 5; AP Photo/Matt Slocum, p. 7; Heinz Kluetmeier/Getty Images, p. 9; AP Photo/Frank Jansky, p. 11; AP Photo, p. 13; George Gojkovich/Getty Images, p. 14; Matt Dirksen/Getty Images, p. 16; Zoonar/alex grichenko/Alamy, p. 19; Michael Reaves/Getty Images, p. 20; AP Photo/Michael Cazares/Cal Sport Media, p. 22; AP Photo/Ross D. Franklin, p. 23.
Design elements: Kwangmoozaa/Getty Images; Andrii Shelenkov/Getty Images; jasonclardy/Getty Images.
Cover: AP Photo/David Zalubowski.

Table of Contents

★ CHAPTER 1 ★

Becoming the Cubs

On July 4, 2024, Ian Happ stepped up to bat for the Chicago Cubs. He hit a home run!

Happ hit two three-run home runs in the game. The Cubs won!

Chicago won the 1907 and 1908 World Series. But then they didn't win the World Series again for over 100 years.

The Cubs finally won the World Series in 2016. Fans celebrated the big win.

★ CHAPTER 2 ★

Big Moments

Cubs history is full of great plays. The Cubs play at Wrigley Field.

Wrigley Field added lights in 1988. The Cubs beat the New York Mets 6–4 in the stadium's first night game.

In the 2016 World Series, Chicago beat Cleveland in seven games.

It was Chicago's first World
Series win in 108 years.

★ CHAPTER 3 ★

Best Players

The Cubs have had many great players. Ernie Banks played with the Cubs for his entire MLB career.

He hit 512 home runs.
Fans called him Mr. Cub.

Sammy Sosa played most of his career with the Cubs. His 609 career home runs are the ninth most by any player.

In 1998, pitcher Kerry Wood tied the MLB record for most strikeouts in a game. He struck out 20 batters.

Since 1957, the Gold Glove Award has been given to the best fielders in MLB.

In 2024, Ian Happ won his third Gold Glove Award. He is the first Cubs outfielder to win the award three years in a row.

★ CHAPTER 4 ★

Go, Cubs, Go!

Fans love to watch games at Wrigley Field.

Wrigley is the second-oldest MLB ballpark. The Cubs began playing there in 1916.

Cubs games are full of fun moments.

The Cubs haven't returned to the World Series since 2016. But fans are hopeful that they will soon.

The Cubs have many good players. The team has a lot to be excited about.

CHICAGO CUBS TEAM LEADERS

Batting average: Bill Madlock, .336

Hits: Cap Anson, 3,012

Home runs: Sammy Sosa, 545

Wins: Charlie Root, 201

Strikeouts: Fergie Jenkins, 2,038

Glossary

fielder: a baseball player who plays defense

home run: a hit that allows the batter to run around all the bases and score

MLB: Major League Baseball

strikeout: an out after the batter has gotten three strikes

Learn More

Downs, Kieran. *Baseball*. Bellwether Media, 2024.

Leed, Percy. *Baseball: A First Look*. Lerner Publications, 2023.

Leed, Percy. *Baseball's World Series*. Lerner Publications, 2025.

Index